GWENDOLYN B. BENNETT

NOCTURNES & OTHER VERSE

FORGOTTEN POETS

Editor | Dick Whyte   Number 16 | 2023

GWENDOLYN B. BENNETT (1902-1981) was born in Giddings, Texas, and spent her early childhood on the Paiute Reservation in Nevada where her parents were teachers, before relocating to Washington, Pennsylvania, and then New York. At a young age Bennett excelled at writing and painting, and would go on to study fne arts and teaching at both Columbia University and the Pratt Institute. Bennett published her frst 'free verse' in *The Crisis* in 1923, and took a position at Howard University the following year teaching design, watercolour painting, and crafts, before receiving a scholarship to study art in Paris. When she returned in 1926 Bennett resumed her position at Howard, worked as an assistant editor at *Opportunity*, continued to publish poetry, wrote short-stories and magazine articles, and illustrated numerous covers for both *Opportunity* and *The Crisis*, as well as co-founding the poetry magazine *Fire!*, with Langston Hughes, Zora Neale Hurston, Aaron Douglas, et al. Alongside being a teacher, poet, and artist, Bennett was committed to advancing African American and women's rights through the arts, and was later an administrator on the New York City Works Progress Administration Federal Arts Project.

Publication credits: 'Nocturne' & 'Quatrain I' (*The Crisis*, Nov. 1923); 'To Usward' (May. 1924); 'Heritage' (*Opportunity*, Dec. 1923); 'Wind' (Nov. 1924); 'Purgation' (Feb. 1925); 'On A Birthday' (Sep. 1925); 'Streetlamps in Early Spring' (May 1926); 'Hatred' (June. 1926); 'Lines Written at the Grave of Alexander Dumas' (July 1926); 'Song I' (Oct. 1926); 'To A Dark Girl' (Oct. 1927); 'Epitaph' (March, 1934); 'Song II' & 'Dirge' (*Palms*, Oct. 1926); 'Moon Tonight' (*Gypsy*, 1927); 'Quatrain I & II', 'Secret', 'Advice', 'To A Dark Girl', 'Your Songs', 'Fantasy', 'Lines', 'Hatred', & 'Two Sonnets' (*Caroling Dusk: An Anthology of Verse by Black Poets*, ed. Countee Cullen, 1927); poetic excerpts from Bennett's literary column 'The Ebony Flute' (*Opportunity*, 1926-28); & the short-stories 'Wedding Day' (*Fire!*, 1926) & 'Tokens' (*Ebony & Topaz*, 1927).

Cover & Inside: Bennett - 3 paintings & a drawing from *The Messenger* (1924); 3 drawings, used as covers for *The Crisis* (Dec. 1923; March, 1924; Jan. 1926); Uncredited - woodcut from the dust-jacket of James Weldon Johnson - *The Autobiography of a Colored Man* (1912); Richard Bruce - 'Face' from *Ebony & Topaz* (1927); etc.

FORGOTTEN PRESS
Aotearoa | New Zealand

ISBN: 978-1-991310-26-2 (paperback) • 978-1-991310-27-9 (hardback)
978-1-991310-28-6 (ebook)

Gwendolyn B. Bennett

Nocturnes & Other Verse

Poems

A selection of verses from magazines,
first published 1923-1934.

Wedding Day

Short-story, first published 1926.

Tokens

Short-story, first published 1927.

FORGOTTEN POETS

edited by **Dick Whyte**.

Missing Meters! Lost Lyrics!
Vanished Verses!

FORGOTTENPOETS.COM

GWENDOLYN B. BENNETT

POEMS

"Song is but the essence of the heart."

—Eva Jessye (1927)

*Dedicated to all Negro youth
known and unknown
who have a song to sing,
a story to tell
or a vision
for the sons of earth.*

—G.B.B. (1924)

Nocturne

THIS cool night is strange
   Among midsummer days . . ,
Far frosts are caught
In the moon's pale light,
And sounds are distant laughter
Chilled to crystal tears.

Quatrains

I

BRUSHES and paints are all I have
To speak the music in my soul—
While silently there laughs at me
A copper jar beside a pale green bowl.

II

How strange that grass should sing—
Grass is so still a thing . . .
And strange the swift surprise of snow,—
So soft it falls and slow.

Heritage

I WANT to see the slim palm-trees,
  Pulling at the clouds
With little pointed fingers . . .

I want to see lithe Negro girls,
Etched dark against the sky
While sunset lingers.

I want to hear the silent sands,
Singing to the moon
Before the Sphinx-still face . . .

I want to hear the chanting
Around a heathen fire
Of a strange black race.

I want to breathe the Lotus flow'r,
Sighing to the stars
With tendrils drinking at the Nile . . .

I want to feel the surging
Of my sad people's soul
Hidden by a minstrel-smile.

To Usward

LET us be still
As ginger jars are still
Upon a Chinese shelf.
And let us be contained
By entities of Self . . .
Not still with lethargy and sloth,
But quiet with the pushing of our growth.
Not self-contained with smug identity
But conscious of the strength in entity.

If any have a song to sing
That's different from the rest,
Oh let them sing
Before the urgency of Youth's behest!

For some of us have songs to sing
Of jungle heat and fires,
And some of us are solemn grown
With pitiful desires,
And there are those who feel the pull
Of seas beneath the skies,
And some there be who want to croon
Of Negro lullabies.

We claim no part with racial dearth;
We want to sing the songs of birth!
And so we stand like ginger jars
Like ginger jars bound round
With dust and age;
Like jars of ginger we are sealed
By nature's heritage.

But let us break the seal of years
With pungent thrusts of song,
For there is joy in long-dried tears
For whetted passions of a throng!

Wind

THE wind was a care-free soul
    That broke the chains of earth,
And strode for a moment across the land
With the wild halloo of his mirth.
He little cared that he ripped up trees,
That houses fell at his hand,
That his step broke calm on the breast of seas,
That his feet stirred clouds of sand.

But when he had had his little joke,
Had shouted and laughed and sung,
When the trees were scarred, their branches broke,
And their foliage aching hung,
He crept to his cave with a stealthy tread,
With rain-filled eyes and low-bowed head.

Purgation

YOU lived
  and your body
Clothed the flames of earth.

Now that the fires have burned away
And left your body cold,
I tremble as I stand
Before the chiseled marble
Of your dust-freed soul.

On a Birthday

ANGELS, craving for a lark
    Rubbed the stars to make a spark,
Pelted lake and sea with pearls
Just to see them break in swirls,
Combed the hair of hill-top trees
Just to hear their singing breeze,
Whispered low to birds on wing
Just to hear them trill and sing,
Laughed to see the summer go,
Reveled in the song of snow,
Played with bird and flower and hill
To find their souls were thirsting still. . . . .

And then they took the spark of star,
The swirl of sea, the pearls from far,
The song of tree and birds in flight,
The shout of sun, the calm of night,
The urge that makes the Winter pass,
The poetry of sighing grass,
The hush of snow, the laugh of rain,
The ache of joy, the pool of pain,
The sunshine and the shadow, too—

They mixed them well and fashioned you!

Street Lamps in Early Spring

NIGHT wears a garment
   All velvet soft, all violet blue . . .
And over her face she draws a veil
As shimmering fine as floating dew . . .
And here and there
In the black of her hair
The subtle hands of Night
Move slowly with their gem-starred light.

Hatred

I SHALL hate you
   Like a dart of singing steel
Shot through still air
At even-tide.
Or solemnly
As pines are sober
When they stand etched
Against the sky.
Hating you shall be a game
Played with cool hands
And slim fingers.
Your heart will yearn
For the lonely splendor
Of the pine tree;
While rekindled fires
In my eyes
Shall wound you like swift arrows.
Memory will lay its hands
Upon your breast
And you will understand
My hatred.

Lines Written at the Grave
of Alexander Dumas

CEMETERIES are places for departed souls
   And bones interred,
Or hearts with shattered loves.
A woman with lips made warm for laughter
Would find grey stones and silent thoughts
Too chill for living, moving pulses . . .
And thou great soul, would shiver
      in thy granite shroud,
Should idle mirth or empty talk
Disturb thy tranquil sleeping.

A cemetery is a place for shattered loves
And broken hearts . . .
Bowed before the crystal chalice of thy soul,
I find the multi-colored fragrance of thy mind
Has lost itself in Death's transparency.

Oh, stir the lucid waters of thy sleep
And coin for me a tale
Of happy loves and gems and joyous limbs
And hearts where love is sweet!

A cemetery is a place for broken hearts
And silent thoughts . . .
And silence never moves, not speaks
    Nor sings.

Song I

I AM weaving a song of waters,
  Shaken from firm, brown limbs,
Or heads thrown back in irreverent mirth
My song has the lush sweetness
Of moist, dark lips
Where hymns keep company
With old forgotten banjo songs
Abandon tells you
That I sing the heart of a race
While sadness whispers
That I am the cry of a soul . . .

A-shoutin', in de ole camp-meetin' place,
A-strummin' o' de ole banjo.
Singin' in de moonlight,
Sobbin' in de dark.
Singin', sobbin', strummin' slow . . .
Singin' slow; sobbin' low.
Strummin', strummin', strummin' slow . . .

Words are bright bugles
That make the shining for my song,
And mothers hold brown babes
To dark, warm breasts
To make my singing sad.

A dancing girl with swaying hips
Sets mad the queen in a harlot's eye.
      Praying slave
      Jazz-band after
      Breaking heart
      To the time of laughter . . .
Clinking chains and minstrelsy
Are welded fast with melody.
      A praying slave
      With a jazz-band after . . .
      Singin' slow, sobbin' low.
Sun-baked lips will kiss the earth.
Throats of bronze will burst with mirth.
      Sing a little faster,
      Sing a little faster,
      Sing!

Song II

OH, my sweet,
    I shall paint you a picture
And call it spring . . . .
Cool greens and sheep
Upon a smoke-blue hill,
And now and then
A puff of snow-white cloud.
I shall write you a poem
And call it spring, too—
A poem of soft, warm words
With little shocks of bright delight . . . .
Deep in the center
Of my inmost self
There sleeps a song—
A laughing tune
Of trills and rhymes . . . .

The hidden song is such a silly thing,
But I shall name it—very softly—SPRING!

Dirge

BURY the love you bore for me
    Deep beneath your laughing songs.
Cover it well with melody;
Let it lie where its ghost belongs.

Laughter was what you had given me,
That and joyous songs to rue.
Cover your love with melody,
For so it thrived and grew.

To a Dark Girl

I LOVE you for your brownness
   And the rounded darkness of your breast.
I love you for the breaking sadness in your voice
And shadows where your wayward eye-lids rest.

Something of old forgotten queens
Lurks in the lithe abandon of your walk
And something of the shackled slave
Sobs in the rhythm of your talk.

Oh, little brown girl, born for sorrow's mate,
Keep all you have of queenliness,
Forgetting that you once were slave,
And let your full lips laugh at Fate!

Moon Tonight

MOON tonight,
   Beloved . . . . .
When twilight
Has gathered together
The ends
Of her soft robe
And the last bird-call
Has died.

Moon tonight—
Cool as a forgotten dream,
Dearer than lost twilights
Among trees where birds sing
No more.

Secret

I SHALL make a song like your hair . . .
   Gold-woven with shadows green-tinged,
And I shall play with my song
As my fingers might play with your hair.
Deep in my heart
I shall play with my song of you . . .

Gently . . .
I shall laugh
At its sensitive lustre . . .
I shall wrap my song in a blanket,
Blue like your eyes are blue
With tiny shots of silver.

I shall wrap it caressingly,
Tenderly . . .
I shall sing a lullaby
To the song I have made
Of your hair and eyes . . .
And you will never know
That deep in my heart
I shelter a song of you
Secretly . . .

Advice

YOU were a sophist,
    Pale and quite remote,
As you bade me
Write poems—
Brown poems
Of dark words
And prehistoric rhythms . . .
Your pallor stifled my poesy
But I remembered a tapestry
That I would some day weave
Of dim purples and fine reds
And blues
Like night and death—
The keen precision of your words
Wove a silver thread
Through the dusk softness
Of my dream-stuff . . .

Your Songs

WHEN first you sang a song to me
    With laughter shining from your eyes,
You trolled your music liltingly
With cadences of glad surprise.

In after years I heard you croon
In measures delicately slow
Of trees turned silver by the moon
And nocturnes sprites and lovers know.

And now I cannot hear you sing,
But love still holds your melody
For silence is a sounding thing
To one who listens hungrily.

Fantasy

I SAILED in my dreams to the Land of Night
   Where you were the dusk-eyed queen,
And there in the pallor of moon-veiled light
The loveliest things were seen . . .

A slim-necked peacock sauntered there
In a garden of lavender hues,
And you were strange with your purple hair
As you sat in your amethyst chair
With your feet in your hyacinth shoes.

Oh, the moon gave a bluish light
Through the trees in the land of dreams and night.
I stood behind a bush of yellow-green
And whistled a song to the dark-haired queen . . .

Sonnets

I

HE came in silvern armour, trimmed with black—
A lover come from legends long ago—
With silver spurs and silken plumes a-blow,
And flashing sword caught fast and buckled back
In a carven sheath of Tamarack.

He came with footsteps beautifully slow,
And spoke in voice meticulously low.
He came and Romance followed in his track . . .

I did not ask his name—I thought him Love;
I did not care to see his hidden face.
All life seemed born in my intaken breath;
All thought seemed flown like some forgotten dove.
He bent to kiss and raised his visor's lace . . .
All eager-lipped I kissed the mouth of Death.

II

SOME things are very dear to me—
  Such things as flowers bathed by rain
Or patterns traced upon the sea
Or crocuses where snow has lain . . .
The iridescence of a gem,
The moon's cool opalescent light,
Azaleas and the scent of them,
And honeysuckles in the night.
And many sounds are also dear—
Like winds that sing among the trees
Or crickets calling from the weir
Or Negroes humming melodies.

But dearer far than all surmise
Are sudden tear-drops in your eyes.

Ebony Flute
[excerpts]

THE wee kiddies
  and the summer-jaded teachers
are again starting their year's work . . .
there's bustle in the air
on the first day of school . . .
but out in the fields
the golden rod is yellow
    and the corn
        is turning brown . . .

And so another moon has passed
and the world do move . . .

The cherry blossoms are blooming . . .
Just the other day
I passed the miracle of
a magnolia tree alight
with blossoming candles.

Epitaph

WHEN I am dead, carve this upon my stone:
Here lies a woman, fit root for flower and tree,
Whose living flesh, now mouldering round the bone,
Wants nothing more than this for immortality,
That in her heart, where love so long unfruited lay
A seed for grass or weed shall grow,
And push to light and air its heedless way;
That she who lies here dead may know
Through all the putrid marrow of her bones
The searing pangs of birth,
While none may know the pains nor hear the groans
Of she who lived with barrenness upon the earth.

GWENDOLYN B. BENNETT

STORIES

WEDDING DAY

Fire! (1926)

HIS name was Paul Watson and as he shambled down rue Pigalle he might have been any other Negro of enormous height and size. But as I have said, his name was Paul Watson. Passing him on the street, you might not have known or cared who he was, but any one of the residents about the great Montmartre district of Paris could have told you who he was as well as many interesting bits of his personal history. He had come to Paris in the days before colored jazz bands were the style. Back home he had been a prize fighter. In the days when Joe Gans was in his glory Paul was following the ring, too. He didn't have that fine way about him that Gans had and for that reason luck seemed to go against him. When he was in the ring he was like a mad bull, especially if his opponent was a white man. In those days there wasn't any sympathy or nicety about the ring and so pretty soon all the ring-masters got down on Paul and he found it pretty hard to get a bout with anyone. Then it was that he worked his way across the Atlantic Ocean on a big liner—in the days before colored jazz bands were the style in Paris.

Things flowed along smoothly for the first few years with Paul's working here and there in the unfrequented places of Paris. On the side he used to give boxing lessons to aspiring youths or gymnastic young women. At that time he was working so steadily that he had little chance to find out what was going on around Paris. Pretty soon, however, he grew to be known among the trainers and managers began to fix up bouts for him. After one or two successful bouts a little fame began to come into being for him. So it was that after one of the prize-fights, a colored fellow came to his dressing room to congratulate him on his success as well as invite him to go to Montmartre to meet "the boys."

Paul had a way about him and seemed to get on with the colored fellows who lived in Montmartre and when the first Negro jazz band played in a tiny Parisian cafe Paul was among them playing the banjo. Those first years were without event so far as Paul was concerned. The members of that first band often say now that they wonder how it was that nothing happened during those first seven years, for it was generally known how great was Paul's hatred for American white people. I suppose the tranquility in the light of what happened afterwards was due to the fact that the cafe in which they worked was one in which mostly French people drank and danced and then too, that was before there were so many Americans visiting Paris. However, everyone had heard Paul speak of his intense hatred of American white folks. It only took two Benedictines to make him start talking about what he would do to the first "Yank" that called him "nigger." But the seven years came to an end and Paul Watson went to work in a larger cafe with a larger band, patronized almost solely by Americans.

I've heard almost every Negro in Montmartre tell about the night that a drunken Kentuckian came into the cafe where Paul was playing and said:

"Look heah, Bruther, what you all doin' ovah heah?"

"None ya bizness. And looks here, I ain't your brother, see?"

"Jack, do you heah that nigger talkin' lak that tah me?"

As he said this, he turned to speak to his companion. I have often wished that I had been there to have seen the thing happen myself. Every tale I have heard about it was different and yet there was something of truth in each of them. Perhaps the nearest one can come to the truth is by saying that Paul beat up about four full-sized white men that night besides doing a great deal of damage to the furniture about the cafe. I couldn't tell you just what did happen. Some of the fellows say that Paul seized the nearest table and mowed down men right and left, others say he took a bottle, then again the story runs that a chair was the instrument of his fury. At any rate, that started Paul Watson on his seige against the American white person who brings his native prejudices into the life of Paris.

It is a verity that Paul was the "black

terror." The last syllable of the word, nigger, never passed the lips of a white man without the quick reflex action of Paul's arm and fist to the speaker's jaw. He paid for more glassware and cafe furnishings in the course of the next few years than is easily imaginable. And yet, there was something likable about Paul. Perhaps that's the reason that he stood in so well with the policemen of the neighborhood. Always some divine power seemed to intervene in his behalf and he was excused after the payment of a small fine with advice about his future conduct. Finally, there came the night when in a frenzy he shot the two American sailors.

They had not died from the wounds he had given them hence his sentence had not been one of death but rather a long term of imprisonment. It was a pitiable sight to see Paul sitting in the corner of his cell with his great body hunched almost double. He seldom talked and when he did his words were interspersed with oaths about the lowness of "crackers." Then the World War came.

It seems strange that anything so horrible as that wholesale slaughter could bring about any good and yet there was something of a smoothing quality about even its baseness. There has never been such equality before or since such as that which the World War brought. Rich men fought by the side of paupers; poets swapped yarns with dry-goods salesmen, while Jews and Christians ate corned beef out of the same tin. Along with the general leveling influence came France's pardon of her prisoners in order that they might enter the army. Paul Watson became free and a French soldier. Because he was strong and had innate daring in his heart he was placed in the aerial squad and cited many times for bravery. The close of the war gave him his place in French society as a hero. With only a memory of the war and an ugly scar on his left cheek he took up his old life.

His firm resolutions about American white people still remained intact and many chance encounters that followed the war are told from lip to lip proving that the war and his previous imprisonment had changed him little. He was the same Paul Watson to Montmartre as he shambled up rue Pigalle.

Rue Pigalle in the early evening has a sombre beauty—gray as are most Paris streets and other-worldish. To those who know the district it is the Harlem of Paris and rue Pigalle is its dusky Seventh Avenue. Most of the colored musicians that furnish Parisians and their visitors with entertainment live somewhere in the neighborhood of rue Pigalle. Some time during every day each of these musicians makes a point of passing through rue Pigalle. Little wonder that almost any day will find Paul Watson going his shuffling way up the same street.

He reached the corner of rue de la Bruyere and with sure instinct his feet stopped. Without half thinking he turned into "the Pit." Its full name is The Flea Pit. If you should ask one of the musicians why it was so called, he would answer you to the effect that it was called "the pit" because all the "fleas" hang out there. If you did not get the full import of this explanation, he would go further and say that there were always "spades" in the pit and they were as thick as fleas. Unless you could understand this latter attempt at clarity you could not fully grasp what the

Flea-Pit means to the Negro musicians in Montmartre. It is a tiny cafe of the genus that is called distro in France. Here the fiddle players, saxophone blowers, drum beaters and ivory ticklers gather at four in the afternoon for a porto or a game of billiards. Here the cabaret entertainers and supper musicians meet at one o'clock at night or thereafter for a whiskey and soda, or more billiards. Occasional sandwiches and a "quiet game" also play their parts in the popularity of the place. After a season or two it becomes a settled fact just what time you may catch so-and-so at the famous "Pit."

The musicians were very fond of Paul and took particular delight in teasing him. He was one of the chosen few that all of the musicians conceded as being "regular." It was the pet joke of the habitues of the cafe that Paul never bothered with girls. They always said that he could beat up ten men but was scared to death of one woman.

"Say fellow, when ya goin' a get hooked up?"

"Can't say, Bo. Ain't so much on skirts."

"Man alive, ya don't know what you're missin'—somebody little and cute telling ya sweet things in your ear. Paris is full of women folks."

"I ain't much on 'em all the same. Then too, they're all white."

"What's it to ya? This ain't America."

"Can't help that. Get this—I'm collud, see? I ain't got nothing for no white meat to do. If a woman eva called me nigger I'd have to kill her, that's all!"

"You for it, son. I can't give you a thing on this Mr. Jefferson Lawd way of lookin' at women."

"Oh, tain't that. I guess they're all right for those that wants 'em. Not me!"

"Oh you ain't so forty. You'll fall like all the other spades I've ever seen. Your kind falls hardest."

And so Paul went his way—alone. He smoked and drank with the fellows and sat for hours in the Montmartre cafes and never knew the companionship of a woman. Then one night after his work he was walking along the street in his queer shuffling way when a woman stepped up to his side.

"Voulez vous."

"Naw, gowan away from here."

"Oh, you speak English, don't you?"

"You an 'merican woman?"

"Used to be 'fore I went on the stage and got stranded over here."

"Well, get away from here. I don't like your kind!"

"Aw, Buddy, don't say that. I ain't prejudiced like some fool women."

"You don't know who I am, do you? I'm Paul Watson and I hate American white folks, see?"

He pushed her aside and went on walking alone. He hadn't gone far when she caught up to him and said with sobs in her voice:—

"Oh, Lordy, please don't hate me 'cause I was born white and an American. I ain't got a sou to my name and all the men pass me by cause I ain't spruced up. Now you come along and won't look at me cause I'm white."

Paul strode along with her clinging to his arm. He tried to shake her off several times but there was no use. She clung all the more desperately to him. He looked down at her frail body shaken with sobs, and something caught at his heart.

Before he knew what he was doing he had said:—

"Naw, I ain't that mean. I'll get you some grub. Quit your cryin'. Don't like seein' women folks cry."

It was the talk of Montmartre. Paul Watson takes a woman to Gavarnni's every night for dinner. He comes to the Flea Pit less frequently, thus giving the other musicians plenty of opportunity to discuss him.

"How times do change. Paul, the woman-hater, has a Jane now."

"You ain't said nothing, fella. That ain't all. She's white and an 'merican, too."

"That's the way with these spades. They beat up all the white men they can lay their hands on but as soon as a gang of golden hair with blue eyes rubs up close to them they forget all they ever said about hatin' white folks."

"Guess he thinks that skirt's gone on him. Dumb fool!"

"Don' be no chineeman. That old gag don' fit for Paul. He cain't understand it no more'n we can. Says he jess can't help himself, everytime she looks up into his eyes and asks him does he love her. They sure are happy together. Paul's goin' to marry her, too. At first she kept saying that she didn't want to get married cause she wasn't the marrying kind and all that talk. Paul jus' laid down the law to her and told her he never would live with no woman without being married to her. Then she began to tell him all about her past life. He told her he didn't care nothing about what she used to be jus' so long as they loved each other now. Guess they'll make it."

"Yeah, Paul told me the same tale last night. He's sure gone on her all right."

"They're gettin' tied up next Sunday. So glad it's not me. Don't trust these American dames. Me for the Frenchie."

"She ain't so worse for looks, Bud. Now that he's been furnishing the green for the rags."

"Yeah, but I don't see no reason for the wedding bells. She was right—she ain't the marrying kind."

. . . and so Montmartre talked. In every cafe where the Negro musicians congregated Paul Watson was the topic for conversation. He had suddenly fallen from his place as bronze God to almost less than the dust.

The morning sun made queer patterns on Paul's sleeping face. He grimaced several times in his slumber, then finally half-opened his eyes. After a succession of dream-laden blinks he gave a great yawn, and rubbing his eyes, looked at the open window through which the sun shone brightly. His first conscious thought was that this was the bride's day and that bright sunshine prophesied happiness for the bride throughout her married life. His first impulse was to settle back into the covers and think drowsily about Mary and the queer twists life brings about, as is the wont of most bridge-grooms on their last morning of bachelorhood. He put this impulse aside in favor of dressing quickly and rushing downstairs to telephone Mary to say "happy wedding day" to her.

One huge foot slipped into a worn bedroom slipper and then the other dragged painfully out of the warm bed were the courageous beginnings of his bridal toilette. With a look of triumph he put on his new grey suit that he had ordered from an English tailor. He carefully pulled a taffeta tie into place beneath his chin, noting as he looked at his face in the mirror that the scar he had received in the army was very ugly—funny, marrying an ugly man like him.

French telephones are such human faults. After trying for about fifteen minutes to get Central 32.01 he decided that he might as well walk around to Mary's hotel to give his greeting as to stand there in the lobby of his own, wasting his time. He debated this in his mind a great deal. They were to be married at four o'clock. It was eleven now and it did seem a shame not to let her have a minute or two by herself. As he went walking down the street towards her hotel he laughed to think of how one always cogitates over doing something and finally does the thing he wanted to in the beginning anyway.

* * *

Mud on his nice gray suit that the English tailor had made for him. Damn —gray suit—what did he have a gray suit on for, anyway. Folks with black faces shouldn't wear gray suits. Gawd, but it was funny that time when he beat up that cracker at the Periquet. Fool couldn't shut his mouth he was so surprised. Crackers—damn 'em—he was one nigger that wasn't 'fraid of 'em. Wouldn't he have a hell of a time if he went back to America where black was black. Wasn't white nowhere, black wasn't. What was that thought he was trying to get ahold of—bumping around in his head—something he started to think about but couldn't remember it somehow.

The shrill whistle that is typical of the French subway pierced its way into his thoughts. Subway—why was he in the subway—he didn't want to go any place. He heard doors slamming and saw the blue uniforms of the conductors swinging on to the cars as the trains began to pull out of the station. With one or two strides he reached the last coach as it began to move up the platform. A bit out of breath he stood inside the train and looking down at what he had in his hand he saw that it was a tiny pink ticket. A first class ticket in a second class coach. The idea set him to laughing. Everyone in the car turned and eyed him, but that did not bother him. Wonder what stop he'd get off—funny how these French said descend when they meant get off—funny he couldn't pick up French—been here so long. First class ticket in a second class coach!—that was one on him. Wedding day today, and that damn letter from Mary. How'd she say it now, "just couldn't go through with it," white women just don't marry colored men, and she was a street woman, too. Why couldn't she have told him flat that she was just getting back on her feet at his expense. Funny that first class ticket he bought, wish he could see Mary—him a-going there to wish her "happy wedding day," too. Wonder what that French woman was looking at him so hard for? Guess it was the mud.

TOKENS

Ebony & Topaz (1927)

HIGH on the bluff of Saint Cloud stands the Merlin Hospital, immaculate sentinel of Seraigne... Seraigne with its crazy houses and aimless streets, scrambling at the foot of Saint Cloud's immense immutability. Row on row the bricks of the hospital take dispassionate account of lives lost or found. It is always as though the gay, little town of Seraigne were thumbing its nose at Saint Cloud with its famous Merlin Hospital where life is held in a test-tube, a thing to be caught or lost by a drop or two of this or a pellet of that. And past the rustic stupidity of Seraigne's gaiety lies the wanton unconcern of the Seine, Lhe Seine... mute river of sorrows... grim concealer of forgotten secrets... endlessly flowing... touching the edges of life... moving purposefully along with a grey disdain for the empty, foolish paiety of Seraigne or the benign dignity of Merlin Hospital, high on the warm cliffs of Saint Cloud.

A trim nurse had drawn Jenks Barnett's chair out onto one of the balconies that over-looked the Seine. Listlessly, aimlessly he turned his thoughts to first one aspect and then another of the Seine, Merlin Hospital, the cliffs of Saint Cloud, Seraigne . . . over and again . . . the Seine, Merlin Hospital, the cliffs . . . of . . . Saint . . . Cloud . . . silly, little Seraigne. It was a better way—that Seine business. Just swallow up life and sorrow and sadness . . . don't bother about the poor fools who are neither dead nor alive . . . just hanging on to the merest threads of existence . . . coughing out one's heart and yet somehow still keeping heart. Purposeless thoughts these as one just as purposelessly fingers the blanket that covers one's emaciated, almost lifeless legs. But the Seine goes on, and Seraigne continues to be happy, and the pain in one's chest grows no easier.

It so happened that at this particular time there were a number of colored patients at the Merlin Hospital. Most of them were musicians who had remained in Paris after the World War. Two of them had come to London and thence to Paris with Will Marion Cook in the Negro entertainer's hey-day. Jenks was one of these. He had been a singer in those days. His voice was now spoken of in the hushed tones one uses when speaking of the dead. He had cherished great plans for himself in those days and no one dared hope otherwise, so rare was his voice in range and quality. That was all changed now...

Merlin Hospital had won nation-wide fame as a haven for patients suffering from tuberculosis. An able staff of doctors and nurses administered daily hope of recovery to broken bodies or perhaps kindly, although inadequate, solace to those whose cases were hopeless. Jenks Barnett had been there five weeks. His case was one of the hopeless ones. The tale of his being there did not take long in the telling. Shortly after the success of Cook's orchestra with its inimitable "singing trombonist" Tollie had come—Tollie Saunders with her golden voice and lush laughter. From the very first she and Jenks had hit it off well together. It was not long before he was inextricably enmeshed in the wonder of her voice and the warm sweetness of her body. Dinner at Les Acacias... for Tollie... a hat for her lovely head... that dress in Chanal's window . . . she wanted one of those large opal rings... long nights of madness under the charm of her flute-sweet voice. His work began to suffer. Soon he was dismissed from the orchestra. Singing soirees didn't pay too well. And then one day before the pinch of poverty came Tollie had left him, taking with her all the pretty things he had given her... leaving no farewell... her chance had come to sing in an American production and she had gone. No word of their plan to startle the singing world with their combined talents; no hint of regret that she was leaving...just gone. Three nights on a gorgeous drunk and he had awakened to find himself in a dingy, damp Parisian jail with a terrific pain in his back... eighteen days in which he moved from one prison-house to another ... sunshine and air again when his friends had finally found him and arranged for his release... sunshine lasts but a short time in Paris . . . endless days of splashing

through the Paris rain in search of a job...
always that pain between his shoulder-
blades...then night upon night of blowing
a trombone in a stuffy little Botte de Nuit
during which time he forgot the pain in
his back...and drink...incessant drink...
one more drink with the fellows...and
after the job cards and more drink.
One came to Merlin after one had been to
the American Hospital. One came to
Merlin after one had been to every other
hospital round about Paris. It does not
take long to become accustomed to the
turning knife in one's chest. It is good for
a hopeless case to watch the uncurbed
forgetfulness of the Seine.

Spring had sent ahead its perfume this
day. It was as though the early March air
were powdered with the pollen of many
unborn flowers. A haze settled itself in the
air and on the breast of the river. Jenks
forgot for a moment the relentless ache in
his bosom and breathed deeply in sheer
satisfaction. In the very midst of this
gesture of aliveness the tool of death,
lodged in his lung, gave a wrench. A
hacking cough rose in his throat and then
seemed to become stuck there. His great,

gaunt frame was shaken in a paroxysm of pain. The fit of stifled coughing over, his head fell back upon the pillow. A nurse hurried to his side. "Guess you'd better go in now. I told you not to move around."

With quick, efficient hands she tucked the cover more closely about his legs, lowered the back of the invalid chair in which he was sitting, and pushed him carefully back into the hospital. As his chair was rolled through the ward it was as though he were running the gamut of scorn. Jenks was not a favorite at the hospital by any stretch of the imagination. Few of the patients there had escaped the lash of his tongue. Sour at life and the raw deal it had dealt him, he now turned his attention to venting his spume on those about him. Nurses, doctors, orderlies, fellow-patients, persistent friends . . . all shared alike the blasphemy of his words. Even Bill Jackson, the one friend who continued to brave the sting of his vile tongue, was not spared. Bill had known him and loved him before Lollie came. It was in this memory that he wrapped himself when Jenks was most unbearable. He accused Bill of stealing his money when he asked him to bring him something from the city...There had been many who had tried to make Jenks' last days easier but one by one they had begun to stay away until now there was only Bill left. Little wonder the other patients in the hospital heaped invective upon him as he passed.

So thin he was as he lay beneath the covers of the bed that his knees and chest made scarcely perceptible mounds in the smooth whiteness of the bed. The brown of his face had taken on the color of dried mud. Great seams folded themselves in his cheeks. There he lay, the rotting hulk of what he had once been. He had sent for Bill . . . these waiting moments were so long!

"Hi there, Jenks"...it was Bill's cheery voice..."thought you'd be outside."

"Can't go out no more. Nearly kicked off the other day."

"Thas all right . . . you'll come around all right."

"For God sakes cut it out. I know I'm done for. You know it, too, damn it all."

"Come on now, fella, be your age. You can't last long if you get yourself all worked up. Take it easy."

"Oh I get so damned sick of the whole business I wish I would hurry up and die. But whose business is that but mine...got somethin' to tell you."

"Shoot."

"See I'm dyin'...get me. They keep stickin' that needle in me but I know damn well I'm dyin'. Now what I want you to do is this...I wrote a letter to Tollie when I first came here...it's in her picture in my suit-case...you know that silver frame. Well when I die I want you to give it to her, if it's a thousand years from now... just a token of the time when we were in love. Don't forget it. Then you remember that French kid that used to be on the ward downstairs...she always liked that radium clock of mine. She's been transferred to the Gerboux Sanitarium... almost well now. I think they said she would be out in a year. Good kid...used to climb up here every afternoon...Stairs sort of wore her out, too. Give her my clock and tell her I hope she lives to be well and strong 'cause I never'll make it. God, she was an angel if ever there was one...she used to sit there on that chair where you're sittin' now and just look at me and say how she wished she could die in my place cause I was such a big man... and could sing so...I believe she'd like to have something to remember me by. And, Bill, you take...that...mmmghgummmm ...mmm..."

That strangling cough rose in his throat. His eyes, always cruel, seemed to look out softly at Bill. A nurse hurried swiftly into the room and injected a hypodermic needle into his arm. A tremor went through his body. His eye-lids half closed...he slept.

The days dragged out in one week after another. Jenks lingered on like the days. Outside the Seine flowed endlessly on unhindered and free. It was all so futile and strange...waiting this way.

June had laid her warm mouth upon the face of the earth. With soft languor the sun slid tenderly over the cliffs of Saint Cloud...even tenderly over the grey bricks of Merlin Hospital. Jenks had raged so about not being allowed to lie on the balcony that at last the hospital authorities had relented...there was such a short time left for him anyway...he might as well have what he wanted . . . this was the first day that had been warm enough. As he lay there he looked out across the cliffs, past the little town of Seraigne, out past the Seine . . . on . . . on . . . immune to life . . . conversant with death . . . on to the great simplicities. He got to thinking of when he was a boy . . . the songs he used to sing . . . he almost thought he'd try to sing now . . . what did it matter if he got another coughing spell . . . but then the nurses would all be in a flurry. Nice to be out here once more looking at the Seine and the world where people lived and breathed.

Bill sighed as he placed the little clock on the mantle-piece. Funny world, this! The French girl had died in late May. He had better not tell Jenks . . . it might upset him. No-o-ope better just keep the clock here. Funny how the first kind thing Jenks had done for anybody since Tollie left him should be done for a person who was dead.

High on the bluff of Saint Cloud stands the Merlin Hospital, immaculate sentinel of Seraigne . . . with its crazy houses and aimless streets, scrambling at the foot of Saint Cloud's immense

immutability. Row on row the bricks of
the hospital take dispassionate account of
lives lost or found.

This Space for Your Thoughts

THE OLD EXPRESSIONS ARE WITH US ALWAYS
AND THERE ARE ALWAYS OTHERS

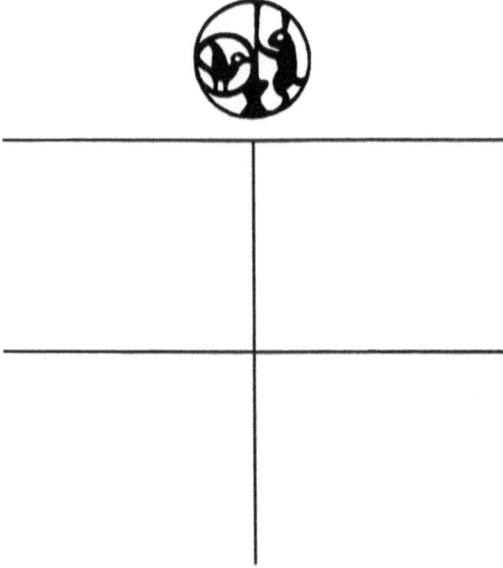

Please handle with care.